LONGHORN BEETLES
of the British Isles

NORMAN HICKIN

CONTENTS

COVER: *Callidium violaceum, adult beetle.*

Series editors: Jim Flegg and Chris Humphries.

Set in 9 point Times roman and printed in Great Britain by C. I. Thomas & Sons (Haverfordwest) Ltd, Press Buildings, Merlins Bridge, Haverfordwest, Dyfed.

Introduction

Insects are by far the most numerous animals on earth, comprising about seventy per cent of all species. The number of species so far described has been variously estimated between 277,000 and 350,000. About forty per cent of all described insects are beetles and about a third of all animals are beetles. Yet a study of the basic characteristics of beetles, their external anatomy, physiology and so on, provides no obvious clue as to the reason for their great biological success.

Beetles are mainly characterised by possessing only one pair of wings (metathoracic), which are folded up, when not in use, under a pair of horny wing cases, or *elytra,* which are anatomically the modified first pair of wings (mesothoracic). The elytra fit tightly together down the middle line of the body and it has been suggested that this feature may account for the great success of beetles. This is because most of the

breathing pores, or *spiracles* along the body are situated in a cavity between the top surface of the abdomen, which is membranous, and the horny elytra and this would be of great importance in conservation of water.

All beetles are placed in the order Coleoptera, which is divided into four suborders: Archostemata, Myxophaga, Adephaga and Polyphaga. The suborder Polyphaga, which has nearly 25,000 species worldwide, is divided into 96 families, which are grouped in eighteen superfamilies. Within the Polyphaga, the longhorns are a family of easily identified beetles formerly known as the Longicornia but now called the Cerambycidae, in the superfamily Chrysomeloidea. They are considered to be among the most highly evolved of beetles.

Most of the longhorn beetles do not have common English names and so are referred to by their scientific names. The Cerambycidae, like all other families, is subdivided into genera (singular: genus), which are the smallest groups of related species. The scientific name of an insect consists of two words. The first word is

1. Typical cerambycid beetle, showing the main parts. From above.

2. Typical cerambycid beetle, showing the main parts. From below.

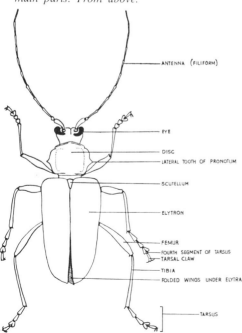

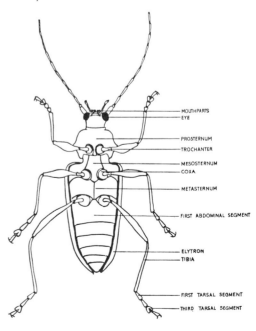

the name of the genus and is spelt with a capital initial letter. The second word is the name of the species and it always begins with a small letter. The name is usually printed in italics. No two genera are given the same name but the specific names may be duplicated in a different genus. Thus the combination of the generic name and the individual specific name identifies only one particular species and, furthermore, its relationship with a group of species can be seen at once. In scientific work the name of the person who first described the species should follow the name, either in full or in an abbreviated form. This is not necessary in an introductory work like the present one.

This system of naming plants and animals, named the Linnaean system after its founder, the Swedish botanist Carl Linnaeus (1707-78), has been universally adopted and it has enabled the naming of insects to be conducted in an exact manner. Complications and anomalies sometimes arise but generally the system works very well.

The Cerambycidae is a well defined family of which about twenty thousand species have been described worldwide. They are found throughout the world wherever trees or bushes grow and indeed wherever timber is transported or used. The number of British indigenous species is usually given as rather more than sixty. F. A. J. Duffy lists 64 but gives a further 46 species found as larvae in imported timber. The number of species in tropical areas is very much greater than in temperate regions. C. F. C. Beeson states that over twelve hundred are known from the Indian sub continent and of these two hundred were described as new from 1914 to 1941. No doubt this list is now much longer and will grow for many years. Duffy describes the larvae of, or makes reference to, 603 species from the African region but remarks that many thousands of African species are known. In America also there is a multiplicity of species, especially in South America. Some are of gigantic proportions and often they are of remarkable form and colour.

Generally longhorn beetles are of medium size but some such as *Macroto-*

3. *Part side-view of the head of an adult longhorn beetle showing base of antennae and lunate compound eye made up of a number of separate lenses.*

ma heros and *Titanus giganteus* are amongst the largest known insects, with a size considerably greater than that of a small mammal. Other species are very small and a few are minute. The form of the beetle is fairly well defined, although there is wide variation. The body is usually elongate with the wing cases wider than the pronotum. The most characteristic feature of the longhorns, however, shared by all but a few species (and referred to in their name), is the extreme length of the antennae. These are usually as long as, or longer than, the body. In *Batocera kibleri* they reach a length of 24 cm (9 inches). The eyes are large and frequently bow-shaped, caused by the large tubercle from which the antenna arises. The antennae are usually thread-like (filiform) but sometimes, as in the British species *Prionus coriarius*, they are saw-like (serrate). They are occasionally also comb- or feather-shaped (pectinate) and sometimes they are ornamented with tufts of hair. One important character possessed by the antennae of all species is that they can be held backwards along the length of the body.

The legs of longhorns, are quite large and in a few species the front (prothoracic) legs are extended to an exaggerated degree, both the femur and the tibia being as long as the body or even longer. In every case there are five tarsal segments although the fourth segment is

3

very small and only four segments are visible to the naked eye, the microscope or a X10 lens being required to find the fifth. The third tarsal segment has a bilobed appearance.

All longhorn larvae are phytophagous (plant-eating) or xylophagous (wood-eating). The great majority feed on the woody tissue of trees and shrubs, but the larvae of some species are found consuming the roots or stems of herbaceous plants and yet others occur only in the pith of young shoots. The extent to which fungal decay occurs in wood determines which longhorn species will feed on it. *Hylotrupes bajulus* will feed on the sapwood of Scots pine(*Pinus sylvestris*) when fungal decay is absent but the dead stumps, heavily infested with fungus, are attacked by *Rhagium* and some other genera. Many longhorn larvae will feed only on one species of host tree but some feed on a wide range of tree species. Again some feed only in the sapwood whilst others feed on the cambium layer (see below). Beeson notes that the tree *Shorea robusta* from tropical Asia is the host to no fewer than 38 longhorn species, whereas the longhorn *Stromatium barbatum* is known to feed on 311 tree species.

THE BIOLOGY OF WOOD

A high proportion of the larval and pupal stages are spent in wood either in twigs or branches or in the trunks of trees. Some explanation of the terms commonly used is therefore given here in order that the significant differences between the biologies of the different species may be understood.

Some species prefer *softwoods,* which are the cone-bearing or coniferous trees (Gymnosperms), and others prefer *hardwoods,* the broad-leaved trees (Angiosperms). Examples of softwoods are fir, pine, spruce and larch and hardwoods include oak, elm, ash, birch, chestnut and walnut. This definition is important because many tropical hardwoods are actually softer than many softwoods and, on the other hand, there are several hard softwoods.

In both softwoods and hardwoods the wood is differentiated into an outer layer of *sapwood* and the inner core of *heart-wood.* In many timbers there is a great difference between the heartwood and the sapwood but in others heartwood and sapwood may be identified only with difficulty. There is, however, an important biological significance; only the sapwood contains living tissue and only in this outer layer of wood is watery sap transported throughout the trunk and branches. The heartwood consists of dead tissues only, and into it is often excreted matter no longer required by the tree for the living processes. It is often the deposition of waste matter which alters the colour or the texture of the heartwood and its durability and many other properties.

The bark of the tree is divided into the outer bark, which is dead tissue, and the inner bark, or *bast,* which contains living tissue. Between the inside of the bast and the outside of the sapwood lies the very important *cambium* layer, which is usually moist or slimy in the living tree. The tree produces new sapwood cells on the inside of the cambium and new bast cells on the outside. The cambial layer is often a preferred location for the development of the young larval longhorns.

The centre of the trunk or branch, at the position of the first growth ring, is known as the *pith.*

Biology and life cycle

THE HOUSE LONGHORN

Amongst all the longhorn species in Europe there is one that is an important pest of timber. This is the House Longhorn Beetle *(Hylotrupes bajulus).* It should not be confused with two other insect species, the Woodworm and the Deathwatch Beetle, which are also serious pests of timber but are not longhorns. The species generally known as Woodworm is a small chocolate-brown beetle only about 3 mm (0.1 inch) in length. The larva is hook-shaped and the external flight-hole is circular and about 1.5 mm (0.06 inch) in diameter. The other wood-boring species,

4

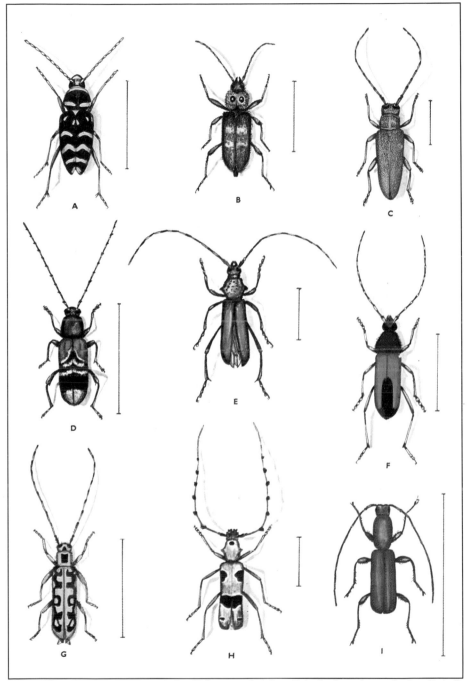

4. A. *Plagionotus arcuatus* (L.) B. *Hylotrupes bujulus* (L.) C. *Saperda carcharias* (L.) D. *Anaglyptus mysticus* (L.) E. *Aromia moschata* (L.) F. *Purpuricenus hochleri* (L.) G. *Saperda scalaris* (L.) H. *Rosalia alpina* (L.) I. *Gracilia minuta* (Fabricius) Length of line = 12 mm in each case except 'I' (Gracilia minuta) in which it is 6 mm.

5

popularly called Deathwatch, is found only in hardwoods, generally oak and chestnut in which fungal decay occurs to some degree. The beetle is about 5 to 7 mm (0.25 inch) in length, dark brown, with the body covered with small yellowish scales when freshly emerged but which quickly get rubbed off. The larva is hook-shaped and the circular flight hole is about 3 to 4 mm (0.1 inch) in diameter.

Hylotrupes bajulus is commonly known as the *Hausbock* in Germany, where its biology has been the subject of more research than that of any other insect species, with a view to its destruction. Its life cycle is therefore described here as an example, although other species may differ in various respects.

The House Longhorn almost certainly originated in North Africa. It is now distributed from central Norway to North Africa and from Portugal to Siberia. In addition, it was introduced and established itself in many other countries including Australia, South Africa and the United States. After a vigorous campaign it was eliminated from Australia and very stringent rules are now applied to prevent it being re-introduced.

It has been known in Britain since 1795. It is probable that in the late nineteenth century it was widespread, infesting softwood in houses, but since the early 1930s it has been confined in Britain to north-west Surrey, south-west London and a restricted area on the Sussex coast. A number of instances are recorded of larvae being imported in packing cases and orange boxes. This seems to be the most likely source of recent sporadic infestations.

In Britain House Longhorn is confined to the timber of conifers of the genera *Pinus, Picea* and *Abies* (pine, spruce and fir) although in continental Europe the larvae have been recorded on *Alnus, Corylus* and *Quercus* (alder, hazel and oak). The sapwood of the dry timber is infested and not until the greater part of this is repeatedly tunnelled does the larva bore into the heartwood. The first timber in a building to be infested is usually that in the roofspace and various theories have been put forward to account for this, the most often quoted being that this

situation is very hot in summer, but perhaps the alternation of cold in winter is of equal importance. The general spread of House Longhorn in Europe in recent years has been explained by the replacement of thatch by slates, tiles and bituminised felt, all of which absorb heat whilst thatch has a heat-insulating effect. The part of Britain where the species is established is in the area of the country with the highest summer temperature.

COURTSHIP AND EGG LAYING
In warm weather the adult female House Longhorn produces chemical substances known as pheromones which attract the male, activate the male genitalia and cause the female to be receptive. Courtship is often vigorous: legs and antennae often get bitten off in the process. Immediately after copulation the female searches for a suitable egg-laying site. She appears to be attracted by the smell of terpenes, which are a group of strong-smelling chemicals from which turpentine is produced and which are derived from resinous wood. She then searches for cracks of a suitable size in the wood. These would be about 0.25 to 0.6 mm (0.01 to 0.024 inch) wide, extending 20 to 30 mm (0.8 to 1.2 inch) into the wood. She then elongates the egg-laying tube, or *ovipositor,* pushes it into the chosen site and carefully places an egg, its exact position being determined by finger-like palps at the end of the ovipositor.

Several clutches of eggs are laid over a period of about twelve days. The average number of eggs laid is between 140 and 200. The eggs are dull white and spindle-shaped and are 1.2 to 2 mm (0.05 to 0.08 inch) in length and 0.5 mm (0.02 inch) in width. They hatch in from five and a half to ten days, according to temperatures and relative humidity.

THE LARVA
Within twelve hours of hatching the young larva can burrow into the wood if the surface is rough. In general shape the larva is cylindrical, somewhat flattened, and broadest at the front end — the thorax. It tapers towards the hinder end but then becomes wider again before tapering to the tail end. The colour is a shiny ivory white. There are deep

grooves between the segments. The head is small and its hinder part is retracted into the thorax, but the jaws are powerful and heavily pigmented. The larva is up to 24 mm (0.9 inch) in length and 7.5 mm (0.3 inch) in width and it is oval in transverse cross-section.

The larva has very small but well defined legs although they are probably of little use to it as the abdominal segments enable it to move efficiently within the tunnel. Simple eyes (ocelli) are present on the head near the base of the mandibles; the number varies according to species. Throughout the larval period, except for the first few days when it burrows into the wood, the larva is in the dark so that eyes are of little value. The larva can be clearly heard gnawing, especially in the warm weather when it is most active. The faecal pellets (frass) are cylindrical and when the wood is largely consumed they fill the oval larval borings nearest the surface, which are often discernible as long raised, blister-like protrusions. These sometimes burst, leaving long light-coloured wavy lines on the surface of the wood.

Except for a few resting periods when the skin is changed, the entire larval period is taken up by feeding. The strong laterally disposed jaws pull off groups of wood fibres. Some are rejected (these are often in long strips), but most pass through the alimentary canal. The nutrition of the larva has been studied by several investigators. Symbiotic organisms, such as occur in a number of other wood-eating insects such as Common Woodworm *(Anobium punctatum)* and the *Kalotermes* group of termites, are apparently absent. However, the enzyme cellulase is present and it has been estimated that about twenty per cent of the cellulose and related substances present in the cellwalls of the wood fibres is broken down into simpler materials which can be digested by the larva. Apart from cellulose products small amounts of albumen are a necessity as well as proteins which are present in the dry cell sap.

Other longhorns may differ in their feeding habits from *Hylotrupes bajulus,* especially those that eat decayed wood. The larva usually takes from three to six years to develop but it is not uncommon for it to take only two years or up to ten years and there is one record of 32 years. Both larvae and adults of this species have perforated sheeting of lead or other metals covering wood in order to enter or escape.

THE PUPA
Pupation generally takes place during the spring and only a short distance below the wood surface. The pupa is white, from 14 to 25 mm (0.5 to 1 inch) in length, and all the appendages of the adult are easily discernible under a thin transparent cuticle. The mandibles resemble those of the adult in being pointed. The duration of the pupal stage varies according to conditions from eleven days to 44 days.

THE ADULT
The adult beetles emerge between July and September, usually when the weather is hot. Equal numbers of males and females are produced. The beetle survives as an adult insect for an average of only 25 days. During cold weather it hides in cracks or amongst loose debris but in warm weather it becomes very active, and this is when courtship and mating take place.

Little is known of the range of flight of the adult beetle. Hardly any experimental work using the 'capture and release' technique has been carried out and there are no recorded observations of the beetle in flight in the wild. The beetles do not wander far. The almost worldwide distribution has occurred through commerce, the larvae being carried in the timber used in packing cases. A number of records have occurred in orange boxes imported into Britain.

A number of other longhorn species are known to be strong flyers, especially those frequenting flowers, but they are not often found away from their natural habitat, except for those that may emerge from wood in timber yards and other urban locations.

Adult *Hylotrupes bajulus* do not appear to eat, although other longhorn species are attracted to white and sometimes coloured flowers, where pollen and perhaps nectar are consumed. Flowers

5 (above). *Hylotrupes bajulus. Courtship lasts about one and a half minutes and copulation about the same. Courtship is often violent.*

6 (left). *Hylotrupes bajulus. The eggs are dull white and spindle-shaped and each is carefully placed in a shrinkage crack in the wood.*

7 (below). *Hylotrupes bajulus, larva. The head is inserted into the prothorax. The jaws are very strong.*

8. *Hylotrupes bajulus, pupa. Pupation usually takes place near the surface of the wood.*

The principal British species

Prionus coriarius, one of the largest beetles, reaches 40 mm (1.6 inches) in length and is broad and stout. It is uniformly dull brownish black. The underside of the male is downy but not that of the female. The antennae are sawtoothed and have twelve segments in the male, eleven in the female. It occurs in the southern English counties. The larvae are found in decaying broad-leaved as well as coniferous tree trunks.

Tetropium gabrieli is probably the only indigenous species in this genus of five species. It has black elytra and measures 10 to 15 mm (0.4 to 0.6 inch) long. It is normally found under the bark of felled larch but it sometimes occurs with other coniferous trees. It is an important forestry insect as unhealthy trees may be rapidly destroyed by it. It occurs in southern England.

Criocephalus ferus is found in southern Britain and is generally uncommon, although abundant in some Surrey localities. It is about 20 mm (0.8 inch) long and is found in dead or decaying standing trees or stumps of pine and spruce, especially those scorched by fire. The pupae are active, moving up and down the cell. The adult emerges in July and August.

Criocephalus rusticus occurs in Britain only in eastern Scotland, where it is found in pine stumps. In France it sometimes damages structural woodwork in buildings and will bore through zinc sheeting.

Gracilia minuta is very small, 3.5 to 5 mm (0.1 to 0.2 inch) long, and the antennae of the male are distinctly longer than the body. It is reddish brown. The larvae occur in the dead dry twigs of bramble, dog rose and a number of hedgerow shrubs. They sometimes cause damage to wickerwork.

are often a meeting place of the sexes.

Little is known of the relative sense values of eyes and antennae. Both are well developed. Observations show, however, that sight guides the beetle in the wide environment, such as directing it towards large white blossoms during long sweeping flights. The antennae appear to be used in locating nearby objects, such as for mate selection, orientation during copulation and differentiating between types of wood tissue for egg laying.

Male longhorn beetles die soon after mating and the females when egg laying is completed.

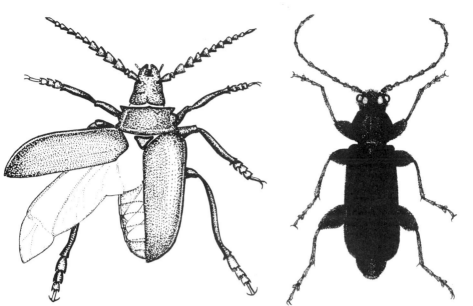

9 (above left). *Prionus coriarius, with elytron lifted to display wing. Length 37 mm (1.5 inch). Larvae live in tree roots of a variety of species.*

10 (above right). *Tetropium gabrieli. Length 11 mm (0.4 inch). Adult beetle usually found under bark of felled larch.*

11 (below left). *Criocephalus ferus. Length 19 mm (0.7 inch). Eyes not hairy (compare C. rusticus with hairy eyes).*

12 (below right). *Cerambyx cerdo. Length 42 mm (1.7 inch). Head and pronotum shining black, elytra brownish near apices.*

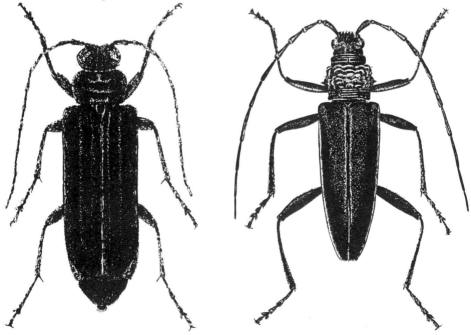

Cerambyx cerdo is one of the larger wood-boring beetles likely to be found in Britain, measuring from 25 to 50 mm (1 to 2 inches). It is not a native species but is commonly imported with oak from Europe and also occurs in a few other hardwoods. The head and pronotum are shining black and the elytra are black also but gradually become reddish brown towards the apices. The adult is nocturnal, being found only at night running over the trunks of old oak trees. It is common generally in Europe. The length of the life cycle is probably two or three years. The larva is often parasitised by the large ichneumon wasp *Rhyssa persuasoria*, which usually attacks the larva of the Wood Wasp. It is recorded also that the larvae of the Goat Moth, *Cossus cossus*, are often found in association with the larvae of *C. cerdo* and the longhorn larva usually comes off worst in an encounter.

Cerambyx scopoli is smaller than *C. cerdo*, being from 16 to 28 mm (0.6 to 1.1 inch) in length. It is entirely black in colour and is generally common in Europe. It is not indigenous to Britain although it is commonly imported in timber. The beetle is found during daytime on flowers of Rosaceae (such as cultivated and dog roses), Umbelliferae (such as hogweed), and elder. The larvae are found in a number of tree species but chiefly beech, cherry, apple and oak. Like *C. cerdo* the life cycle lasts two or three years.

Rhagium bifasciatum is the most widely distributed of the British cerambycids. It occurs throughout England, Scotland and Wales. The elytral marking is extremely variable: seventeen patterns have been named. The larvae are to be found in decaying stumps and logs. They prefer Scots pine but have also been found in fir, spruce, ash, oak, beech, hornbeam, alder, mountain ash and willow.

Rhagium mordax is readily distinguished from other longhorns by the black mark on each elytron and the oblique yellow bands giving an eye-like appearance. The larvae are usually found in the cambium-layer sapwood of rotting boles and stumps of oak but have occurred in a wide variety of broad-leaved and coniferous species. The adult metamorphoses from August but remains in the pupal

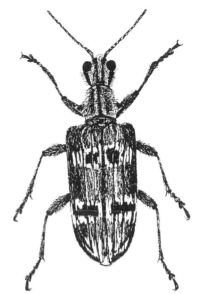

13. *Rhagium inquisitor. Length 14 mm (0.6 inch). Two black marks surrounded by yellow on each elytron.*

14. *Stenocorus meridianus. Length 17 mm (0.7 inch). Elytra black or brown. Larvae feed in stumps of cherry and a few other species.*

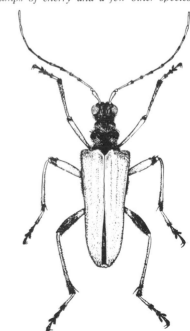

11

15. *Cerambyx cerdo is one of the largest longhorns likely to be found in Britain although not indigenous.*

16. *Molorchus minor. Note the very long antennae and the very short elytra which do not reach halfway down the abdomen. It has a two-year life cycle.*

17. *Pyrrhidium sanguineum could be confused with the beetle Pyrochrou coccinea but the antennae of the latter are pectinate and the former filiform.*

18. *Clytus arietis is one of the best known longhorns in Britain.*

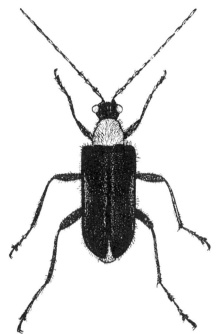

19. *Acmaeops collaris*. Length 6 mm (0.2 inch). Red thorax, elytra bluish-black.

attracted to the flowerheads of hogweed and other Umbelliferae.

Acmaeops collaris is only 7 to 9 mm (0.3 inch) long. The wing cases of this small cerambycid are shining black and covered with hair whilst the thorax is chestnut red. The adults are usually found on flowers in woodland. The larvae are unusual in that they do not appear to make their own tunnel in wood as do all other longhorns but are found in the old tunnels of other cerambycids, where they feed either on old larval frass or associated fungi.

Strangalia maculata is probably the commonest and most widely distributed of all the six species of the genus. It is 15 to 17 mm (0.6 inch) in length and the elytra vary in coloration from almost completely yellow to almost completely black. Generally, however, transverse bands of black give a wasp-like appearance. The legs are long and spidery. The larvae are found in stumps of oak, birch,

20. *Strangalia maculata*. Length 11 mm (0.4 inch). Markings on the elytra are very variable.

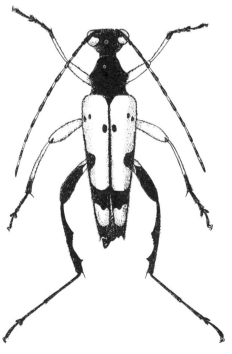

cell until the following spring, so this species can be found every month of the year.

Rhagium inquisitor possesses a pair of black marks surrounded by yellowish bands on each elytron. It has a northern distribution. The larvae feed on the wood of conifers, preferring it less decayed than those of *R. mordax*. This probably accounts for their not infrequent importation in softwoods from North America, adding to the native British population. Both this and the foregoing species are attracted to white objects and settle on them.

Stenocorus meridianus is large but slim, 15 to 24 mm (0.6 to 0.9 inch) in length and very variable. Some beetles are all black but covered with a fine down while others have rusty yellow elytra. The antennae and legs are long and may sometimes be red. A feature of its shape is the narrowing of the elytra towards the apex. It occurs mainly in the south and is fairly local. The larvae are to be found in old stumps of cherry, ash and willow. The adults emerge in May and June and are

14

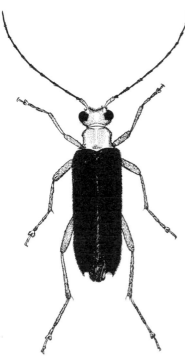

21. *Strangalia revestita. Length 12 mm (0.5 inch). A rare insect. Larvae are said to feed on the wood of bird cherry, Prunus avium.*

22. *Strangalia melanura. Length 9.2 mm (0.4 inch). Inner margins and apices of elytra are black.*

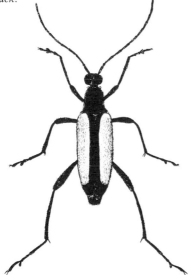

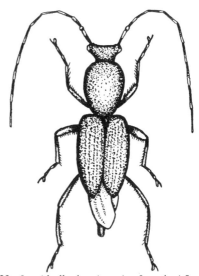

23. *Leptideella brevipennis. Length 4.5 mm (0.2 inch). This small species is found infesting wickerwork (willow) and a number of other hardwood species.*

willow, beech, ash, aspen, sweet chestnut, hornbeam and hazel. The adult is often found on garden flowers such as rose. *S. aurulenta* is a rare insect found only in southern England. The larvae are found in the stumps of a variety of hardwood trees. *S. quadrifasciata* is also rare and its larvae are also found in the stumps of hardwood trees. *S. revestita* is rare and little is known about it. *S. nigra* is 8 to 9 mm (0.3 inch) in length and entirely black in colour. The flying adults are attracted to blossoms of wood spurge. *S. melanura* shows differences in colouring between the sexes. The thorax is black and the elytra are dark reddish yellow in the male but in the female the apical and central parts of the elytra are marked in black.

Leptideella brevipennis is a very small species — only 6 mm (0.2 inch) or so in length. Formerly it was imported from time to time from continental Europe in wickerwork but it has now been established in England for some years. The larvae are found in dead dry twigs of willow and dog rose. On the continent they are found in many hardwood and some softwood species. The elytra do not entirely cover the abdomen and the head is constricted in the neck area.

24. *Phymatodes testaceus, adult. At one time this species was local in southern England but after the Second World War it became very common. Today it is again much less abundant because oak is now stored in an unbarked condition.*

Molorchus minor is about 10 mm (0.4 inch) in length and the elytra are very small, scarcely covering half of the abdomen and the folded wings. The antennae are about twice the length of the insect. The larvae are found in damaged or recently cut branches of pine, spruce, larch and birch. It has a two-year life cycle and although the final metamorphosis takes place in August and September the adult beetles remain in the pupal cell until the following May or June. It is found locally in England south of Yorkshire. *M. umbellatarum* is very rare, the larvae being found in various hedgerow shrubs.

Aromia moschata, the Musk Beetle, is a gem amongst the British longhorns, but as the name suggests it emits a strong odour. It is 20 to 30 mm (0.8 to 1.2 inch)

25. *Phymatodes testaceus, larva. The larval galleries are packed with frass and often loosen the bark from the wood in heavy infestations. A two-year life cycle is usual.*

in length. The whole body including the legs and antennae is normally a beautiful metallic green but may be bluish or even bright blue. It is widely distributed throughout the British Isles but is local. The antennae of males are one and a half times the length of the body but those of females are shorter than the body. The larvae feed on the decaying wood of willow. When a tree supports a population it usually does so for many years and should be rigorously conserved.

Phymatodes testaceus, the Oak Long-horn, is usually abundant and at one time was a serious pest of oak floors. Although it prefers the sapwood of oak, it also affects chestnut, beech, willow and a few other timbers. Only the sapwood is tunnelled and only in the unbarked condition. The lifecycle usually takes two years. The adult is remarkable for occurring in two distinct colour phases. In one the elytra are yellowish

26 (right). *Gracilia minuta is found chiefly in dead twigs, wattle hurdle and wickerwork.*
27 (below). *Pogonocherus hispidus has a variable pattern of small white hairs and black spine-like bristles over the body and legs, giving a banded appearance. It is locally distributed throughout the British Isles.*

brown and in the other deep black-blue. The insect measures from 8 to 13 mm (0.3 to 0.5 inch). *P. lividus* is occasionally imported from continental Europe. *P. alni* is found in the recently dead twigs and branches (including fence posts) of oak, alder, elm, rose, chestnut and ash, the first two being preferred. The elytra of the adult are barred with whitish lunate marks and body length is about 7 mm (0.3 inch). The larvae bore straight tunnels along the sapwood or in the pith canal, where pupation takes place. The adults emerge in April and May.

Callidium violaceum is deep blue-black in colour with attractive violet and mauve reflections. It is flattish in appearance and 12 to 13 mm (0.5 inch) in length. The larvae occur in dry coniferous timber to which the bark is still adhering and out of doors, such as in fence posts. The older larvae do not bore a narrow tunnel or gallery but excavate a flat oval area in the sapwood. The life cycle takes two years. The standing trees are not attacked.

Pyrrhidium sanguineum is a very beautiful red longhorn with a flattened appearance. There is a superficial similarity to the cardinal beetles (*Pyrochroa coccinea* and *P. serraticornis* in the family Pyrochroidae), both in colour and size. In the two latter species, however, the antennae are comb-like but in the longhorn they are thread-like. As an indigenous insect it appears to be confined to Herefordshire but elsewhere it is introduced from time to time and is quickly noticed on account of its colour. It is associated mainly with oak. It measures 10 to 12 mm (0.4 inch).

Clytus arietis is perhaps the best known of the longhorn beetles in Britain, being generally common throughout the British Isles. The transverse black and yellow banding and quick wasp-like movements make it easily observed in the garden. The long hind legs distinguish it from the rarer *Plagionotus arcuatus*. The body is about 14 mm (0.6 inch) in length. A variety of host hardwood timbers have been recorded. Until the larva is about half-grown it feeds entirely just underneath the bark but thereafter it tunnels into the sapwood, where finally the pupal cell is constructed. Usually only dead

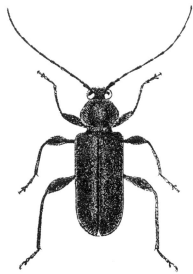

28. *Callidium violaceum. Length 12 mm (0.5 inch). Deep blue-black with violet and mauve spots. Larvae feed in softwoods, mainly sapwood and inner bark.*

29. *Pyrrhidium sanguineum. Length 11 mm (0.4 inch). Legs, antennae and body are black but red coloration caused by thick coating of fine red hairs.*

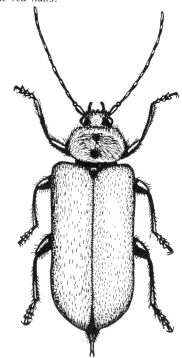

trees, dry fallen branches, garden rustic work or dead parts of living trees are attacked. A number of instances are known where the beetle has emerged from beech furniture indoors. The life cycle is usually of two years duration.

Pogonocherus fasciculatus is one of three British members of the genus. They are all small and are characterised by the apex of the elytra having the appearance of being cut off transversely. Body length is 5 to 7 mm (0.2 inch) with a characteristic pattern, as have also the other two species. The larva has been found in dead twigs of fir. *P. hispidulus* is the second species, with large pale areas on the elytra, and the third is *P. hispidus*, which occurs amongst ivy. These two species possess pointed projections at the apices of the elytra.

Acanthocinus aedilis is known as the Timberman. It is characterised by the extraordinary length of the antennae: in the male they are four times the body length, but only twice the body length in the female. The latter, however, possesses an extremely long ovipositor. The body is from 13 to 19 mm (0.5 to 0.7 inch) long and is reddish, covered with greyish

30. *Pogonocherus hispidulus. Length 7.5 mm (0.3 inch). Larvae in applewood and other hardwoods. Local but widely distributed.*

31. *Pogonocherus hispidus. Length 6 mm (0.2 inch). Larvae in dead or decaying twigs of a wide range of hardwoods and also mistletoe.*

32. *Acanthocinus aedilis. Left: female. Right: male. Length 18 mm (0.7 inch), without ovipositor. Known as the Timberman. A northern insect. The larvae are found in softwoods.*

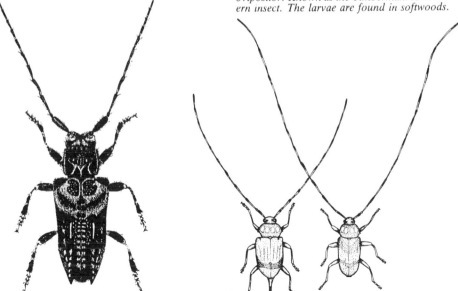

33. *Mesosa nebulosa. The pitch-black ground colour of the insect is almost completely covered with a pattern of dense greyish, reddish yellow and white short hairs. The species is found in southern and eastern England.*

down. It has a mainly northern distribution, being found chiefly in Scotland and Ireland, but it is often imported in pine and fir.

Agapanthia villosoviridescens is moderately large and elongate, 14 mm (0.6 inch) in length. The basic colour of the integument is black but it has a central longitudinal band of fine yellow hairs, which also form lateral bands on the head and pronotum and small patches on the elytra. It is not a wood borer but the larva lives within the main stem of thistle (*Carduus*) or hogweed (*Heracleum*), two

34. *Plagionotus arcuatus. The black and yellow coloration, as well as its agility, gives it a wasp-like appearance.*

per stem. The larva is unusual, being reminiscent of a moth or butterfly caterpillar. It occurs in southern England but is rare.

Saperda carcharias is one of three species in this genus in Britain, all of which are mainly found in willows and poplars. *S. carcharias* is from 20 to 28 mm (0.8 to 1.1 inch) in length. It is black with thick yellow or greyish down having a variable pattern of black markings. It occurs around old willows and poplars. *S. populnea* is 9 to 14 mm (0.4 to 0.6 inch) long. It is yellow and black in colour and is a southern species. *S. scalaris* is 13 to 18 mm (0.5 to 0.7 inch) long and has a ladder-like pattern of black and yellowish green, making it one of the most attractive of longhorn species.

Oberea oculata is 16 mm (0.6 inch) in length and elongate in appearance. The head and elytra are black and the prothorax is brownish orange spotted with black. It is found in the eastern counties of Britain and is very local. The host tree is willow, eggs being laid on the smooth bark of healthy twigs.

Stenostyla ferrea is about 13 mm (0.5 inch) in length and elongate in appearance. The basic colour is black with a greenish blue sheen but there is a covering of greyish white down. The larva feeds in the freshly cut small branches of lime, willow and aspen. The adult beetles feed on the leaves of lime.

Phytoecia cylindrica is dullish black in colour, elongate in appearance and is about 10 mm (0.4 inch) in length. This species is similar to *Agapanthia villosoviridescens* in that the larval life is spent in the stem of certain species of Umbelliferae, including hogweed. It is confined to a few localities in the Midlands and southern England.

INTRODUCED SPECIES

The following are some of the longhorn species that are sometimes introduced into Britain.

Eburia quadrigeminata is known as the American Oak Longhorn. It measures about 20 mm (0.8 inch) in length and is a pale brownish straw colour with two pairs of white marks on each elytron. The antennae are as long as the body or slightly longer. The beetle occasionally emerges from furniture or cabinet woodwork constructed of timber originating from North America. The flight holes are large and oval. In its country of origin it bores into a number of tree species but as oak is the commonest imported timber it is usually seen to emerge from that source. The young larvae gain access to the standing mature oak tree by way of wounds and scars when the bark has been removed. This insect exhibits to a marked degree the phenomenon of delayed development. When the timber is converted and seasoned, the young larva survives and later emerges from fabricated furniture sometimes after an almost unbelievable interval. The records vary from five to forty years. In North America the life cycle takes two or more years and the beetles emerge in summer.

Rosalia alpina is from 20 to 30 mm (0.8 to 1.2 inch) in length, with long antennae half as long again as the body. The sides of the elytra are parallel. The background colour is bluish grey, often with a violet sheen, and the thorax and elytra are patterned with black marks which are ringed with white, three small spots on the thorax and three transverse bands on the elytra. The middle one is large, completely crossing the elytra, but the other bands do not meet in the centre. It is found in the mountainous parts of southern Europe and is known as the *Alpenbock* in Germany. The larvae are found in a number of timber species but beech appears to be preferred, especially if some decay is present. The larvae, however, can feed in sound wood and are known to emerge from structural timber in buildings and from furniture. They are introduced into Britain from time to time in timber.

Purpuricenus hochleri is large, being from 15 to 20 mm (0.6 to 0.8 inch) in length. The head and thorax are black whilst the elytra are carmine red with a central black longitudinal mark. Antennae of the male are slightly longer than the body but those of the female scarcely as long. It is a very attractive insect, sometimes introduced into Britain.

Tetropium fuscum attacks pine and spruce but not usually larch. It is sometimes imported from Europe. The elytra are reddish brown. *T. castaneum* is

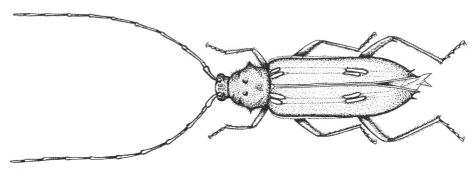

35. *Eburia quadrigeminata. Length 18 mm (0.7 inch). Sometimes imported in hardwoods from North America, mostly in American oak, emerging from furniture after a number of years.*

also introduced into Britain from Europe. Its elytra are also reddish brown. *T. cinnamopterum* has a biology very like *T. gabrieli* but is imported with coniferous timber from North America. It too has reddish brown, elytra. *T. velutinum* comes into Britain from Canada with spruce timber. The elytra are reddish brown.

Ergates faber is a European and North African species imported from time to time into Britain. Sometimes, however, complete life cycles have occurred in a British timber yard. Specimens are known up to 58 mm (2.3 inches) in length. The male has a black head, pronotum and legs and reddish brown elytra whilst the female is uniformly black. The larvae occur only in coniferous timber and do very much better if fungal decay is present. The life cycle takes four or five years to complete and the beetle has been known to bore through lead in order to escape after emergence. Another large species, *E. spiculatus*, is sometimes imported in timber of the species *Pinus ponderosa* and *Pseudotsuga mucronata* from North America.

THE BRITISH SPECIES OF LONGHORNS (CERAMBYCIDAE)

Prionus coriarius	*Leptura rubra*	*Plagionotus arcuatus*
Asemum striatum	*Leptura scutellata*	*Anaclyptus mysticus*
Tetropium gabrieli	*Leptura sanguinolenta*	*Lamia textor*
Criocephalus ferus	*Judolia sexmaculata*	*Monochamus rosenmulleri*
Criocephalus rusticus	*Judolia cerambyciformis*	*Monochamus sartor*
Cerambyx cerdo	*Strangalia revestita*	*Monochamus sutor*
Cerambyx scopolii	*Strangalia aurulenta*	*Monochamus galloprovincialis*
Gracilia minuta	*Strangalia quadrifasciata*	*Monochamus titillator*
Obrium cantharinum	*Strangalia maculata*	*Mesosa nebulosa*
Obrium brunneum	*Strangalia melanura*	*Pogonocherus hispidulus*
Rhagium bifasciatum	*Strangalia nigra*	*Pogonocherus hispidus*
Rhagium mordax	*Leptideella brevipennis*	*Pogonocherus fasciculatus*
Rhagium inquisitor	*Molorchus minor*	*Leiopus nebulosus*
Stenocorus meridianus	*Molorchus umbellatarum*	*Acanthocinus aedilis*
Acmaeops collaris	*Aromia moschata*	*Agapanthia villosoviridescens*
Grammoptera ustulata	*Phymatodes testaceus*	*Saperda carcharias*
Grammoptera holomelina	*Phymatodes alni*	*Saperda populnea*
Grammoptera ruficornis	*Phymatodes lividus*	*Saperda scalaris*
Grammoptera variegata	*Callidium violaceum*	*Oberea oculata*
Alosterna tabacicolor	*Pyrrhidium sanguineum*	*Stenostola ferrea*
Leptura sexguttata	*Hylotrupes bajulus*	*Phytoecia cylindrica*
Leptura livida	*Clytus arietis*	*Tetrops praeusta*
Leptura fulva		

The ecology of longhorns

A number of longhorn species damage sound wood. One such species is *Clytus arietis*, the Wasp Beetle, one of the very few longhorn beetles with a common name. Although not normally infesting household furniture, it will sometimes complete its development and emerge from wood which has been converted and manufactured. The same happens with *Eburia quadrigeminata*. In this case the timber, a softwood, is cut in North America whilst harbouring a few larvae. After importation into Britain the timber is manufactured into window frames. Then many years afterwards the beetles will emerge. Although in its natural habitat the life cycle is about two years, when the tree is felled and the timber dried the completion of the life cycle can still be accomplished but may take as long as forty years.

On the other hand, many longhorns can be considered beneficial to forestry, because the larvae of some species tunnel into fungally decayed wood and thus help to break up the stumps and rotting trunks and bring this un-productive wood substance back into the earth, where it can provide the nutrients and the water-holding properties for a new generation of forest trees or for some other biotic purpose.

Longhorn larvae comprise one of the favourite foods of the woodpeckers and woodpeckers are specifically adapted to capture them with their very long tongues which are sticky and barbed at the tip. Having first broken open the tunnelled wood with chopping blows with the beak, the bird inserts its long tongue along all the tunnels in turn until it finds and draws out the larvae.

Like butterflies longhorn beetles may be sought on flowers, but unlike butter-flies they do not disappear as soon as the sun ceases to shine. Nor do the beetles fly off at the slightest movement of the observer. This makes it easier for a photographer to select a good position for taking his picture. The beetles seem to prefer white or cream-coloured blossoms and of these Hogweed (*Heracleum sphondylium*) appears to be the most popular. In late spring and early summer longhorns should be looked for along the edges of woodland where hogweed abounds or where other white-blossomed plants such as cow parsley and elder (*Sambucus nigra*) are common. Some of the smaller longhorn species hide amongst the mass of flowers.

In the hot sun it is interesting to station oneself on the edge of old woodland, standing by a patch of hogweed, and watch for longhorns to come in. After a wide sweep, when they can be distinguished from bees and hornets, they make an approach trailing their hind legs; then, after a brief hovering period, they either alight or decide to continue their flight in a wide arc elsewhere. The author has observed three species land on a single hogweed inflorescence: *Rhagium mordax*, *Judolia cerambyciformis* and *Stenocorus meridianus*. Some species , however, are commonly found on red and pink flowers such as roses, especially single varieties, examples being *Clytus arietis*, *Anaglyptus mysticus* and *Strangalia maculata*.

Strangalia nigra is a very rare species and it has the habit of flying to the newly opened lime-green inflorescence of wood spurge (*Euphorbia amygdaloides*), where it mates. The larval foodstuff is unknown.

Collecting and conservation

COLLECTING LONGHORN LARVAE

One of the most interesting ways of collecting longhorns is to introduce your-self to your local timber merchant and ask for his help by letting you have any offcuts or pieces of timber which appear insect-damaged. Usually he will be pleased to get rid of these unusable pieces. You could also supply a few tin boxes for any beetles that have already emerged or grubs that have made their way out. It is essential to note the tree species, when you have access to this information, and the date you collect the wood.

Store the wood in large polythene bags carefully sealed up. Condensation may arise if the wood is very wet or badly damaged by fungus. If it occurs dry the polythene bags out or change them but always look out for emerged insects. In addition to the hoped-for longhorn beetles there may be other insects of interest (the writer once reared an extremely rare fern-eating sawfly, now in the British Museum). Thus one has all the excitement of collecting longhorns from foreign parts without the attendant discomfort and expense.

British species can be collected by the same method but wherever you travel look out for piles of roughly cut logs and branchwood piled ready for sawing for burning indoors. Almost every farmyard possesses such a pile. Especially productive are those piles where old orchards have been removed two, three or even more years before. It is sad for the conservationist that the larvae of many of the finest longhorn beetles are destined to be burnt.

LONGHORN CONSERVATION

Perhaps the greatest enemy of longhorn beetles is the woodburning stove. Many pieces of wood cut from the butt end of an old tree with perhaps a streak of fungal decay running though it end up on the flames. When old hedges are removed by a farmer in order to enlarge a field in the interests of economic husbandry the old stools of hazel, hawthorn, honeysuckle and blackthorn are piled up and burnt at the field's edge. Most people think that a piece of woodland 'tidied up' looks neater than one littered with old stumps, dead branches and decaying trunks but it is in the latter situation that there is the greater number of species, including longhorn beetles. This is anathema to the forester, who rightly believes that leaving timber litter about the woodland is fostering many fungal species.

What is required is a 'longhorn garden' where the life cycles of these large and important beetles can be completed, and repeated, until their contained fauna can be reintroduced into a more natural setting. There is usually a firewood merchant resident near large areas of woodland who collects the wood left behind by the timber merchant who has felled the trees. Ask him to make a separate pile of wood pieces that show oval holes or otherwise have the appearance of being the home of longhorn larvae and then bring them home for your longhorn garden.

ACKNOWLEDGEMENTS
    I wish to thank Dr Siegfried Cymorek for permission to use his colour photographs and Mr Bill Johns for checking and sub-editing.